Contents

Grilled Steak & Blue Cheese Sandwiches

6 to 8 cloves Grilled Garlic (recipe page 45), mashed

4 boneless lean, tender beef steaks, such as beef tenderloin or top loin steaks (4 to 6 ounces each), 1 inch thick
Freshly ground or cracked black pepper

2 medium yellow onions
Olive oil

4 French rolls

½ cup crumbled blue cheese

2 small tomatoes, sliced
Mixed greens

Prepare Grilled Garlic. Spread garlic onto both sides of steaks; season generously with pepper. Slice onions into ½-inch-thick slices; brush lightly with oil. Insert wooden picks into onion slices from edges to prevent separating into rings. (Soak wooden picks in hot water 15 minutes to prevent burning.) Lightly oil hot grid to prevent sticking. Place steaks in center of covered grill over medium-hot KINGSFORD® Briquets; place onion slices around steaks. Grill steaks and onion slices 12 to 15 minutes or until steaks are medium-rare or to desired doneness, turning once. Remove steaks from grill; keep warm. Move onions to center of grill and continue grilling 10 to 15 minutes longer until tender and golden brown. Grill rolls, cut sides down, until toasted. Slice steaks into thin strips. Arrange strips over grilled rolls; top with blue cheese, onions, tomatoes and greens.   *Makes 4 servings*

4

Beef

Beef with Dry Spice Rub

3 tablespoons firmly packed brown sugar
1 tablespoon yellow mustard seeds
1 tablespoon whole coriander seeds
1 tablespoon black peppercorns
4 cloves garlic
1½ to 2 pounds beef top round (London Broil) steak, about 1½ inches thick
Vegetable or olive oil
Salt

Place sugar, mustard seeds, coriander seeds, peppercorns and garlic in blender or food processor; process until seeds and garlic are crushed. Rub beef with oil; pat on spice mixture. Season generously with salt.

Lightly oil hot grid to prevent sticking. Grill beef, on covered grill, over medium-low KINGSFORD® Briquets 16 to 20 minutes for medium-rare or until desired doneness, turning once. Let stand 5 minutes before cutting across the grain into thin diagonal slices.   *Makes 6 servings*

Beef

Rosemary Steak

**4 boneless beef top loin (New York strip)
   steaks (about 6 ounces each)**
2 tablespoons minced fresh rosemary
2 cloves garlic, minced
1 tablespoon extra-virgin olive oil
1 teaspoon grated lemon peel
**1 teaspoon coarsely ground or cracked
   black pepper**
½ teaspoon salt
   Fresh rosemary sprigs

Score steaks in diamond pattern on both sides.
Combine minced rosemary, garlic, oil, lemon peel,
pepper and salt in small bowl; rub mixture onto
surface of meat. Cover and refrigerate at least
15 minutes.

Lightly oil hot grid to prevent sticking. Grill steaks
over medium-hot KINGSFORD® Briquets about
4 minutes per side until medium-rare or to desired
doneness. Cut steaks diagonally into ½-inch-thick
slices. Garnish with rosemary sprigs.

Makes 4 servings

Beef

Teriyaki Glazed Beef Kabobs

1¼ to 1½ pounds beef top or bottom
    sirloin, cut into 1-inch cubes
½ cup bottled teriyaki sauce
1 teaspoon dark sesame oil (optional)
1 clove garlic, minced
8 to 12 green onions
1 or 2 plum tomatoes, cut into slices
    (optional)

Thread beef cubes onto metal or bamboo skewers. (Soak bamboo skewers in water 20 minutes to prevent burning.) Combine teriyaki sauce, sesame oil, if desired, and garlic in small bowl. Brush beef and onions with part of glaze, reserving some for grilling; let beef stand 15 to 30 minutes.

Lightly oil hot grid to prevent sticking. Grill beef, on covered grill, over medium KINGSFORD® Briquets, 6 to 9 minutes for medium doneness, turning several times and brushing with reserved glaze. Add onions and tomatoes, if desired, to grid 3 to 4 minutes after beef; grill until onions and tomatoes are tender. Remove from grill; brush skewers, onions and tomatoes with remaining glaze.
Makes 4 servings

Beef

7

Blue Cheese Burgers with Red Onion

2 pounds ground beef chuck
2 cloves garlic, minced
1 teaspoon salt
½ teaspoon black pepper
4 ounces blue cheese
⅓ cup coarsely chopped walnuts, toasted
1 torpedo (long) red onion *or* 2 small red onions, sliced into ⅜-inch-thick rounds
2 baguettes (each 12 inches long) Olive or vegetable oil

Combine beef, garlic, salt and pepper in medium bowl. Shape meat mixture into 12 oval patties. Mash cheese and blend with walnuts in small bowl. Divide cheese mixture equally; place in centers of 6 meat patties. Top with remaining meat patties; tightly pinch edges together to seal in filling.

Lightly oil hot grid to prevent sticking. Grill patties and onion, if desired, on covered grill, over medium KINGSFORD® Briquets, 10 to 12 minutes or until cooked through (165°F), turning once. Cut baguettes into 4-inch lengths; split each piece and brush cut side with olive oil. Move cooked burgers to edge of grill to keep warm. Grill bread, oil sides down, until lightly toasted. Serve burgers on toasted baguettes.   *Makes 6 servings*

Beef

Jamaican Steak

2 pounds beef flank steak
¼ cup packed brown sugar
3 tablespoons orange juice
3 tablespoons lime juice
3 cloves garlic, minced
1 piece (1½×1 inches) fresh ginger, minced
2 teaspoons grated orange peel
2 teaspoons grated lime peel
1 teaspoon salt
1 teaspoon black pepper
¼ teaspoon ground cinnamon
⅛ teaspoon ground cloves
    Shredded orange peel
    Shredded lime peel

Score both sides of beef.* Combine sugar, juices, garlic, ginger, grated peels, salt, pepper, cinnamon and cloves in 2-quart glass dish. Add beef; turn to coat. Cover and refrigerate beef at least 2 hours. Remove beef from marinade; discard marinade.

Lightly oil hot grid to prevent sticking. Grill beef over medium-hot KINGSFORD® Briquets about 6 minutes per side until medium-rare or to desired doneness. Garnish with shredded orange and lime peels.   *Makes 6 servings*

To score flank steak, cut ¼-inch-deep diagonal lines about 1 inch apart in surface of steak to form diamond-shaped design.

Beef

Vietnamese Grilled Steak Wraps

1 beef flank steak (about 1½ pounds)
Grated peel and juice of 2 lemons
6 tablespoons sugar, divided
2 tablespoons dark sesame oil
1¼ teaspoons salt, divided
½ teaspoon black pepper
¼ cup water
¼ cup rice vinegar
½ teaspoon crushed red pepper
6 (8-inch) flour tortillas
6 red leaf lettuce leaves
⅓ cup lightly packed fresh mint leaves
⅓ cup lightly packed fresh cilantro leaves

Cut beef across the grain into thin slices. Combine lemon peel, juice, 2 tablespoons sugar, sesame oil, 1 teaspoon salt and black pepper in medium bowl. Add beef; toss to coat. Cover and refrigerate at least 30 minutes. Combine water, vinegar, remaining 4 tablespoons sugar and ¼ teaspoon salt in small saucepan; bring to a boil. Boil 5 minutes without stirring until syrupy. Stir in red pepper; set aside.

Remove beef from marinade; discard marinade. Thread beef onto metal or wooden skewers. (Soak wooden skewers in hot water 30 minutes to prevent burning.) Lightly oil hot grid to prevent sticking. Grill beef over medium-hot KINGSFORD® Briquets about 3 minutes per side until cooked through. Grill tortillas until hot. Place lettuce, beef, mint and cilantro on tortillas; drizzle with vinegar mixture. Roll tortillas to enclose filling.

Makes 6 servings

Beef

Stuffed Cheese Burgers

1½ cups shredded Monterey Jack cheese (about 6 ounces)
1 can (2¼ ounces) chopped black olives, drained
⅛ teaspoon hot pepper sauce
1¾ pounds ground beef
¼ cup finely chopped onion
1 teaspoon salt
½ teaspoon black pepper
6 whole wheat hamburger buns
  Butter or margarine, melted

Combine cheese, olives and hot pepper sauce in small bowl; mix well. Divide mixture evenly and shape into 6 balls. Mix ground beef with onion, salt and pepper; shape into 12 thin patties. Place a cheese ball in center of 6 patties and top each with a second patty. Tightly pinch edges of each patty to enclose cheese ball. Lightly oil hot grid to prevent sticking. Grill patties, on covered grill, over medium-hot KINGSFORD® Briquets 5 to 6 minutes on each side or until cooked through (165°F).

Split buns, brush with butter and place cut sides down on grill to heat through. Serve burgers on buns. *Makes 6 servings*

Guadalajara Beef and Salsa

1 bottle (12 ounces) Mexican dark beer*
¼ cup soy sauce
2 cloves garlic, minced
1 teaspoon ground cumin
1 teaspoon chili powder
1 teaspoon hot pepper sauce
4 boneless beef sirloin or top loin strip
   steaks (4 to 6 ounces each)
   Salt and black pepper
   Red, green and yellow bell peppers, cut
   lengthwise into quarters, seeded
   (optional)
   Salsa (recipe page 13)
   Flour tortillas (optional)
   Lime wedges

*Substitute any beer for Mexican dark beer.

Combine beer, soy sauce, garlic, cumin, chili powder and hot pepper sauce in large shallow glass dish or large resealable plastic food storage bag. Add beef; cover dish or seal bag. Marinate in refrigerator up to 12 hours, turning beef several times. Remove beef from marinade; discard marinade. Season with salt and black pepper.

Lightly oil hot grid to prevent sticking. Grill beef and bell peppers, if desired, on covered grill, over medium KINGSFORD® Briquets, 8 to 12 minutes, turning once. Beef should be of medium doneness and peppers should be tender. Serve with salsa, tortillas, if desired, and lime wedges.

Makes 4 servings

Beef

Salsa

- 2 cups coarsely chopped seeded tomatoes
- 2 green onions with tops, sliced
- 1 clove garlic, minced
- 1 to 2 teaspoons minced seeded jalapeño or serrano chili pepper,* fresh or canned
- 1 tablespoon olive or vegetable oil
- 2 to 3 teaspoons lime juice
- 8 to 10 sprigs fresh cilantro, minced (optional)
- ½ teaspoon salt or to taste
- ½ teaspoon sugar or to taste
- ¼ teaspoon black pepper

Jalapeño peppers can sting and irritate the skin; wear rubber gloves when handling peppers and do not touch your eyes. Wash hands after handling peppers.

Combine tomatoes, green onions, garlic, chili pepper, oil and lime juice in medium bowl. Stir in cilantro, if desired. Season with salt, sugar and black pepper. Adjust seasonings to taste, adding lime juice or chili pepper, if desired.

Makes about 2 cups

Western Lamb Riblets

5 pounds lamb riblets, cut into serving-size pieces
¾ cup bottled chili sauce
½ cup beer
½ cup honey
¼ cup Worcestershire sauce
¼ cup finely chopped onion
1 clove garlic, minced
½ teaspoon crushed red pepper flakes

Trim excess fat from riblets. In saucepan, combine chili sauce, beer, honey, Worcestershire sauce, onion, garlic and pepper flakes. Bring mixture to a boil. Reduce heat; simmer, covered, 10 minutes. Remove from heat; cool.

Place riblets in resealable plastic food storage bag. Pour cooled marinade over riblets in bag. Seal bag and refrigerate about 2 hours, turning bag occasionally to distribute marinade evenly.

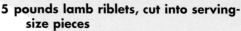

Drain riblets; reserve marinade. Lightly oil hot grid to prevent sticking. Arrange medium-hot KINGSFORD® Briquets around drip pan. Place riblets on grid over drip pan. Cover grill; cook 45 minutes, turning riblets and brushing with marinade twice. Bring remaining marinade to a boil; serve with riblets. *Makes 6 servings*

Lamb

Middle Eastern Kabobs with Cucumber Sauce

1½ cups diced cucumber (about ½ pound)
1 cup plain low-fat yogurt
1 tablespoon lemon juice
1 clove garlic, minced
3 tablespoons minced fresh mint, divided
1 teaspoon salt, divided
2 green onions, chopped
2 teaspoons cornstarch
½ teaspoon ground cumin
¼ teaspoon ground cinnamon
¼ teaspoon black pepper
¼ teaspoon cayenne pepper
1 pound ground lamb,* beef or turkey
1 tablespoon olive oil**

*If ground lamb is unavailable, place 1 pound boneless lamb cubes in food processor; process using on/off pulsing action until lamb is ground.

**Omit olive oil if using beef or turkey.

Combine cucumber, yogurt, lemon juice, garlic, 1 tablespoon mint and ½ teaspoon salt in medium bowl; cover and refrigerate ½ hour. Combine remaining 2 tablespoons mint and ½ teaspoon salt, onions, cornstarch and spices in large bowl. Add lamb and oil; mix well. Form two 2×1½-inch oblong meatballs around each of 4 metal skewers. Grill meatballs on covered grill over medium-hot KINGSFORD® Briquets about 15 minutes until no longer pink, turning to brown all sides. Serve with cucumber sauce. *Makes 4 servings*

Lamb

Pork Tenderloin with Grilled Apple Cream Sauce

1 can (6 ounces) frozen apple juice
  concentrate, thawed and divided
½ cup Calvados or brandy, divided
2 tablespoons Dijon mustard
1 tablespoon olive oil
3 cloves garlic, minced
1¼ teaspoons salt, divided
¼ teaspoon black pepper
1½ pounds pork tenderloin
2 green or red apples, cored
1 tablespoon butter
½ large red onion, cut into thin slivers
½ cup heavy cream

Reserve 2 tablespoons juice concentrate. Combine remaining juice concentrate, ¼ cup Calvados, mustard, oil, garlic, 1 teaspoon salt and pepper in glass dish. Add pork; turn to coat. Cover and refrigerate 2 hours, turning pork occasionally. Cut apples crosswise into ⅜-inch rings. Remove pork from marinade; discard marinade. Grill pork on covered grill over medium KINGSFORD® Briquets about 20 minutes, turning 3 times, until meat thermometer inserted in thickest part registers 155°F. Grill apples about 4 minutes per side until tender; cut rings into quarters. Melt butter in large skillet over medium heat. Add onion; cook and stir until soft. Stir in apples, remaining ¼ cup Calvados, ¼ teaspoon salt and reserved 2 tablespoons juice concentrate. Add cream; heat through. Cut pork crosswise into ½-inch slices; spoon sauce over pork. *Makes 4 servings*

Pork

Peanut Pork Tenderloin

⅓ cup chunky unsweetened peanut butter
⅓ cup regular or light canned coconut milk
¼ cup lemon juice or dry white wine
3 tablespoons soy sauce
3 cloves garlic, minced
2 tablespoons sugar
1 piece (1-inch cube) fresh ginger, minced
½ teaspoon salt
¼ to ½ teaspoon cayenne pepper
¼ teaspoon ground cinnamon
1½ pounds pork tenderloin

Combine peanut butter, coconut milk, lemon juice, soy sauce, garlic, sugar, ginger, salt, cayenne pepper and cinnamon in 2-quart glass dish until blended. Add pork; turn to coat. Cover and refrigerate at least 30 minutes or overnight. Remove pork from marinade; discard marinade.

Lightly oil hot grid to prevent sticking. Grill pork on covered grill over medium KINGSFORD® Briquets about 20 minutes, turning 4 times, until meat thermometer inserted in thickest part registers 155°F. Cut crosswise into ½-inch slices. Serve immediately.   *Makes 4 to 6 servings*

Pork Chops with Apple-Sage Stuffing

6 center-cut pork chops (3 pounds), about 1 inch thick
¾ cup dry vermouth, divided
4 tablespoons minced fresh sage *or* 4 teaspoons rubbed sage, divided
2 tablespoons soy sauce
1 tablespoon olive oil
2 cloves garlic, minced
½ teaspoon black pepper, divided
1 tablespoon butter
1 medium onion, diced
1 apple, cored and diced
½ teaspoon salt
2 cups fresh firm white bread crumbs

Cut pocket in each chop using tip of thin, sharp knife. Combine ¼ cup vermouth, 2 tablespoons fresh sage, soy sauce, oil, garlic and ¼ teaspoon pepper in glass dish; add pork chops, turning to coat. Heat butter in large skillet over medium heat until foamy. Add onion and apple; cook and stir about 6 minutes until onion is tender. Stir in remaining ½ cup vermouth, 2 tablespoons sage, ¼ teaspoon pepper and salt. Cook and stir over high heat about 3 minutes until liquid is almost gone. Transfer onion mixture to large bowl. Stir in bread crumbs.

Remove pork chops from marinade; discard marinade. Spoon onion mixture into pockets of pork chops. Close openings with wooden picks. (Soak wooden picks in hot water 15 minutes to prevent burning.) Grill pork chops on covered grill over medium KINGSFORD® Briquets about 5 minutes per side until barely pink in center.

Makes 6 servings

18

Pork

Pork Chops with Orange-Radish Relish

2 cups orange juice
⅓ cup lime juice
⅓ cup packed brown sugar
3 medium oranges, peeled, seeded and
    cut into ¼-inch pieces
¼ cup chopped red onion
¼ cup diced radishes
2 tablespoons finely chopped fresh
    cilantro
6 pork chops (about ¾ inch thick)
    Salt and black pepper

Combine both juices and brown sugar in saucepan. Cook mixture at a low boil, stirring often, about 20 minutes until reduced to about ½ cup and it has syruplike consistency. Set aside ¼ cup orange syrup for basting.

Meanwhile, prepare Orange-Radish Relish by combining oranges, onion and radishes in colander or strainer and drain well; transfer to bowl. Add cilantro and gently stir in remaining orange syrup. Season pork with salt and pepper.

Lightly oil hot grid to prevent sticking. Grill pork, on covered grill, over medium KINGSFORD® Briquets, 7 to 10 minutes. (Pork is done at 160°F; it should be juicy and slightly pink in center.) Halfway through cooking, brush with reserved ¼ cup orange syrup and turn once. Serve with Orange-Radish Relish.   *Makes 6 servings*

Pork

August Moon Korean Ribs

⅓ **cup water**
⅓ **cup soy sauce**
¼ **cup thinly sliced green onions**
3 **tablespoons dark sesame oil**
3 **tablespoons honey**
2 **tablespoons minced garlic**
2 **tablespoons sesame seeds**
1 **tablespoon grated fresh ginger**
1 **teaspoon black pepper**
3½ **pounds pork back ribs**

To prepare marinade, combine all ingredients except ribs in small bowl. Place ribs in large resealable plastic food storage bag. Pour marinade over ribs, turning to coat. Seal bag. Marinate in refrigerator overnight.

Lightly oil hot grid to prevent sticking. Arrange medium KINGSFORD® Briquets on each side of rectangular metal or foil drip pan. Grill ribs in center of grid on covered grill 35 to 45 minutes or until ribs are browned and cooked through, turning once.   *Makes 8 servings*

Citrus Marinated Chicken

- **1 cup orange juice**
- **¼ cup lemon juice**
- **¼ cup lime juice**
- **2 cloves garlic, pressed or minced**
- **4 boneless skinless chicken breast halves**
  Salt and black pepper
  Citrus Tarragon Butter (recipe page 45)
  Hot cooked couscous with green onion slices and slivered almonds (optional)
  Lemon and lime slices and Italian parsley for garnish (optional)

Combine orange, lemon and lime juices, and garlic in shallow glass dish or large resealable plastic food storage bag. Add chicken; cover dish or seal bag. Marinate in refrigerator no more than 2 hours. (Lemon and lime juice will "cook" the chicken if it's left in too long.) Remove chicken from marinade; discard marinade. Season chicken with salt and pepper.

Lightly oil hot grid to prevent sticking. Grill chicken, on covered grill, over medium KINGSFORD® Briquets, 6 to 8 minutes until chicken is no longer pink in center, turning once. Serve topped with dollop of Citrus Tarragon Butter. Serve over couscous, if desired. Garnish, if desired.   *Makes 4 servings*

Chicken

Hot, Spicy, Tangy, Sticky Chicken

1 chicken (3½ to 4 pounds), cut up
1 cup cider vinegar
1 tablespoon chili powder
1 tablespoon Worcestershire sauce
1 teaspoon salt
1 teaspoon black pepper
1 teaspoon hot pepper sauce
¾ cup KC MASTERPIECE™ Original
    Barbecue Sauce

Place chicken in shallow glass dish or large resealable plastic food storage bag. Combine vinegar, chili powder, Worcestershire sauce, salt, black pepper and hot pepper sauce in small bowl; pour over chicken pieces. Cover dish or seal bag. Marinate in refrigerator at least 4 hours, turning several times.

Lightly oil hot grid to prevent sticking. Place dark meat pieces on grill 10 minutes before white meat pieces (dark meat takes longer to cook). Grill chicken on covered grill, over medium KINGSFORD® Briquets, 30 to 45 minutes, turning once or twice. Turn and baste with KC MASTERPIECE™ Original Barbecue Sauce the last 10 minutes of cooking. Remove chicken from grill; baste with barbecue sauce. Chicken is done when meat is no longer pink near bone.

Makes 4 servings

Chicken

Pesto Chicken & Pepper Wraps

⅔ cup refrigerated pesto sauce or frozen pesto sauce, thawed and divided
3 tablespoons red wine vinegar
¼ teaspoon salt
¼ teaspoon black pepper
1¼ pounds skinless boneless chicken thighs or breasts
2 red bell peppers, cut in half, stemmed and seeded
5 (8-inch) flour tortillas
5 thin slices (3-inch rounds) fresh-pack mozzarella cheese*
5 leaves Boston or red leaf lettuce

*Packaged sliced whole milk or part-skim mozzarella cheese can be substituted for fresh-pack mozzarella cheese.

Combine ¼ cup pesto, vinegar, salt and black pepper in medium bowl. Add chicken; toss to coat. Cover and refrigerate at least 30 minutes. Remove chicken from marinade; discard marinade. Grill chicken over medium-hot KINGSFORD® Briquets about 4 minutes per side until chicken is no longer pink in center, turning once. Grill bell peppers, skin sides down, about 8 minutes until skin is charred. Place bell peppers in large resealable plastic food storage bag; seal. Let stand 5 minutes; remove skin. Cut chicken and bell peppers into thin strips. Spread about 1 tablespoon of remaining pesto down center of each tortilla; top with chicken, bell peppers, cheese and lettuce. Roll tortillas to enclose filling.

Makes 5 servings

Chicken

23

Classic Grilled Chicken

1 whole frying chicken* (3½ pounds), quartered
¼ cup lemon juice
¼ cup olive oil
2 tablespoons soy sauce
2 large cloves garlic, minced
½ teaspoon sugar
½ teaspoon ground cumin
¼ teaspoon black pepper

*Substitute 3½ pounds chicken parts for whole chicken, if desired. Grill legs and thighs about 35 minutes and breast halves about 25 minutes or until chicken is no longer pink in center, turning once.

Rinse chicken under cold running water; pat dry with paper towels. Arrange chicken in 13×9-inch glass baking dish. Combine remaining ingredients in small bowl; pour half of mixture over chicken. Cover and refrigerate chicken at least 1 hour or overnight. Cover and reserve remaining mixture in refrigerator to use for basting. Remove chicken from marinade; discard marinade. Arrange medium KINGSFORD® Briquets on each side of large rectangular metal or foil drip pan. Pour hot tap water into drip pan until half full. Place chicken on grid directly above drip pan. Grill chicken, skin sides down, on covered grill 25 minutes. Baste with reserved mixture. Turn chicken; cook 20 to 25 minutes or until juices run clear and chicken is no longer pink in center.

Makes 6 servings

Chicken

Lemon Herbed Chicken

½ cup butter or margarine
½ cup vegetable oil
⅓ cup lemon juice
2 tablespoons finely chopped parsley
2 tablespoons garlic salt
1 teaspoon dried rosemary, crushed
1 teaspoon dried summer savory, crushed
½ teaspoon dried thyme, crushed
¼ teaspoon cracked black pepper
6 chicken quarters (breast-wing or thigh-drumstick combinations)

Combine butter, oil, lemon juice, parsley, garlic salt, rosemary, summer savory, thyme and pepper in small saucepan. Heat until butter melts. Place chicken in shallow glass dish. Brush with some of sauce. Let stand 10 to 15 minutes.

Lightly oil hot grid to prevent sticking. Place dark meat pieces on grill 10 minutes before white meat pieces (dark meat takes longer to cook). Grill chicken, on uncovered grill, over medium-hot KINGSFORD® Briquets, 30 to 45 minutes for breast quarters or 50 to 60 minutes for leg quarters. Chicken is done when meat is no longer pink near bone and juices run clear. Turn quarters over and baste with sauce every 10 minutes.

Makes 6 servings

Chicken

25

Southwest Chicken

2 tablespoons olive oil
1 clove garlic, pressed
1 teaspoon ground cumin
1 teaspoon chili powder
1 teaspoon dried oregano leaves
½ teaspoon salt
1 pound skinless boneless chicken breast halves or thighs

Combine oil, garlic, cumin, chili powder, oregano and salt; brush over both sides of chicken to coat. Grill chicken over medium-hot KINGSFORD® Briquets 8 to 10 minutes or until chicken is no longer pink in center, turning once. Serve immediately or use in Build a Burrito, Taco Salad or other favorite recipes.   *Makes 4 servings*

Build a Burrito: *Top warm large flour tortillas with strips of Southwest Chicken and your choice of drained canned black beans, cooked brown or white rice, shredded cheese, salsa verde, shredded lettuce, sliced black olives and chopped cilantro. Fold in sides and roll to enclose filling. Heat in microwave oven at HIGH until heated through. (Or, wrap in foil and heat in preheated 350°F oven.)*

Taco Salad: *For a quick one-dish meal, layer strips of Southwest Chicken with tomato wedges, blue or traditional corn tortilla chips, sliced black olives, shredded romaine or iceberg lettuce, shredded cheese and avocado slices. Serve with salsa, sour cream, guacamole or a favorite dressing.*

Chicken

Grilled Chile Chicken Quesadillas

2 tablespoons lime juice
3 cloves garlic, minced
1 tablespoon ground cumin
1 tablespoon chili powder
1 tablespoon vegetable oil
1 jalapeño pepper, minced
1 teaspoon salt
6 skinless boneless chicken thighs
3 poblano peppers, cut in half, stemmed, seeded
2 avocados, peeled and sliced
3 cups (12 ounces) shredded Monterey Jack cheese
12 (8-inch) flour tortillas
1½ cups fresh salsa

Combine lime juice, garlic, cumin, chili powder, oil, jalapeño pepper and salt in small bowl; coat chicken with paste. Cover and refrigerate chicken at least 15 minutes. Grill chicken on covered grill over medium-hot KINGSFORD® Briquets 4 minutes per side until no longer pink in center. Grill poblano peppers, skin sides down, 8 minutes until skins are charred. Place peppers in large resealable plastic food storage bag; seal. Let stand 5 minutes; remove skin. Cut chicken and peppers into strips. Arrange chicken, peppers, avocados and cheese on half of each tortilla. Drizzle with 2 tablespoons salsa. Fold other half of tortilla over filling. Grill quesadillas on covered grill over medium briquets 30 seconds to 1 minute per side until cheese is melted. *Makes 12 quesadillas*

Herbed Butter Chicken

3 tablespoons minced fresh basil
2 teaspoons minced fresh oregano
2 teaspoons minced fresh rosemary
3 tablespoons minced shallots or green onion
2 tablespoons butter, softened
3 cloves garlic, minced
2 teaspoons grated lemon peel
½ teaspoon salt
¼ teaspoon black pepper
4 chicken legs with thighs *or* 1 whole chicken (about 3½ pounds), quartered
1 tablespoon olive oil

Combine herbs, shallots, butter, garlic, lemon peel, salt and pepper in medium bowl. Loosen chicken skin by gently pushing fingers between skin and chicken, keeping skin intact. Gently rub herb mixture under skin of chicken, forcing it into leg section; secure skin with wooden picks. (Soak wooden picks in hot water 15 minutes to prevent burning.) Cover and refrigerate chicken at least ½ hour. Brush chicken with oil. Arrange medium KINGSFORD® Briquets on each side of rectangular metal or foil drip pan.

Lightly oil hot grid to prevent sticking. Grill chicken, skin sides down, in center of grid on covered grill 20 minutes. Turn chicken and cook 20 to 25 minutes or until juices run clear.

Makes 4 servings

Chicken

Chicken Ribbons Satay

½ cup creamy peanut butter
½ cup water
¼ cup soy sauce
4 cloves garlic, sliced
3 tablespoons lemon juice
2 tablespoons packed brown sugar
¾ teaspoon ground ginger
½ teaspoon crushed red pepper flakes
4 skinless boneless chicken breast halves

Combine peanut butter, water, soy sauce, garlic, lemon juice, brown sugar, ginger and pepper flakes in small saucepan. Cook over medium heat 1 minute or until smooth; cool. Remove garlic from sauce; discard. Reserve half of sauce for dipping. Cut chicken lengthwise into 1-inch-wide strips. Thread onto 8 metal or bamboo skewers. (Soak bamboo skewers in water 20 minutes to prevent burning.)

Lightly oil hot grid to prevent sticking. Grill chicken, on covered grill, over medium-hot KINGSFORD® Briquets, 6 to 8 minutes until chicken is no longer pink in center, turning once. Baste with sauce once or twice during cooking. Serve with reserved sauce.   *Makes 4 servings*

Chicken

Herb Garlic Grilled Chicken

¼ cup chopped parsley
1½ tablespoons minced garlic
4 teaspoons grated lemon peel
1 tablespoon chopped fresh mint
1 chicken (2½ to 3 pounds), quartered

Combine parsley, garlic, lemon peel and mint. Loosen skin from breast and thigh portions of chicken quarters by running fingers between skin and meat. Rub some of seasoning mixture evenly over meat under skin, replace skin and rub remaining seasonings over outside of chicken to cover evenly.

Arrange medium-hot KINGSFORD® Briquets on one side of covered grill. Lightly oil hot grid to prevent sticking. Place chicken on grid opposite coals. Cover grill and cook chicken 45 to 55 minutes, turning once or twice. Chicken is done when juices run clear.   *Makes 4 servings*

Chicken

Turkey Teriyaki with Grilled Mushrooms

1¼ pounds turkey breast slices, tenderloins
    or medallions
¼ cup sake or sherry wine
¼ cup soy sauce
3 tablespoons granulated sugar, brown
    sugar or honey

1 piece (1-inch cube) fresh ginger, minced
3 cloves garlic, minced
1 tablespoon vegetable oil
½ pound mushrooms
4 green onions, cut into 2-inch pieces

Cut turkey slices into long 2-inch-wide strips.*
Combine sake, soy sauce, sugar, ginger, garlic
and oil in 2-quart glass dish. Add turkey; turn
to coat. Cover and refrigerate 15 minutes or
overnight. Remove turkey from marinade; discard
marinade. Thread turkey onto metal or wooden
skewers, alternating with mushrooms and green

onions. (Soak wooden skewers in hot water
30 minutes to prevent burning.) Lightly oil hot grid
to prevent sticking. Grill on covered grill over
medium-hot KINGSFORD® Briquets about
3 minutes per side until turkey is cooked through.

Makes 4 servings

Do not cut tenderloins or medallions.

Turkey

31

Turkey Burritos

1 tablespoon ground cumin
1 tablespoon chili powder
1½ teaspoons salt
1½ to 2 pounds turkey tenderloins, cut into ½-inch cubes
Avocado-Corn Salsa (recipe page 33, optional)
Lime wedges
Flour tortillas
Sour cream (optional)
Tomato slices for garnish

Combine cumin, chili powder and salt in cup. Place turkey cubes in shallow glass dish or large resealable plastic food storage bag; pour dry rub over turkey and coat turkey thoroughly. Let turkey stand while preparing Avocado-Corn Salsa. Thread turkey onto metal or bamboo skewers. (Soak bamboo skewers in water 20 minutes to prevent burning.)

Lightly oil hot grid to prevent sticking. Grill turkey, on covered grill, over medium KINGSFORD® Briquets, about 6 minutes or until turkey is no longer pink in center, turning once. Remove skewers from grill; squeeze lime wedges over skewers. Warm flour tortillas in microwave oven, or brush each tortilla very lightly with water and grill 10 to 15 seconds per side. Top with Avocado-Corn Salsa and sour cream, if desired. Garnish with tomato slices. *Makes 6 servings*

Turkey

Avocado-Corn Salsa

2 small to medium-size ripe avocados,
   finely chopped
1 cup cooked fresh corn or thawed
   frozen corn
2 medium tomatoes, seeded and finely
   chopped
2 to 3 tablespoons chopped fresh cilantro
2 to 3 tablespoons lime juice
½ to 1 teaspoon minced hot green chili
   pepper
½ teaspoon salt

Gently stir together all ingredients in medium
bowl; adjust flavors to taste. Cover and refrigerate
until ready to serve.   *Makes about 1½ cups*

Tip: *This recipe is great for casual get-togethers.
Just prepare the fixings and let the guests make
their own burritos.*

Sausage & Wilted Spinach Salad

¼ cup sherry vinegar or white wine vinegar
1 teaspoon whole mustard seeds, crushed
½ teaspoon salt
¼ teaspoon black pepper
2 ears corn, husked
1 large red onion, cut into ¾-inch-thick slices
4 tablespoons extra-virgin olive oil, divided
12 ounces smoked turkey, chicken or pork sausage links, such as Polish, andouille or New Mexico style, cut in half lengthwise
2 cloves garlic, minced
10 cups lightly packed spinach leaves, torn
1 large avocado, peeled and cubed

Combine vinegar, mustard seeds, salt and pepper; set dressing aside. Brush corn and onion with 1 tablespoon oil. Insert wooden picks into onion slices from edges to prevent separating into rings. (Soak wooden picks in hot water 15 minutes to prevent burning.) Grill sausage, corn and onion over medium KINGSFORD® Briquets 6 to 10 minutes until vegetables are crisp-tender and sausage is hot, turning several times. Cut corn kernels from cobs; chop onion and slice sausage. Heat remaining 3 tablespoons oil in small skillet over medium heat. Add garlic; cook and stir 1 minute. Toss spinach, avocado, sausage, corn, onion and dressing in large bowl. Drizzle hot oil mixture over salad; toss and serve immediately.

Makes 4 servings

Turkey

Barbecued Salmon

4 salmon steaks, ¾ to 1 inch thick
3 tablespoons lemon juice
2 tablespoons soy sauce
  Salt and black pepper
½ cup **KC MASTERPIECE™ Original**
   Barbecue Sauce
  Fresh oregano sprigs
  Grilled mushrooms (optional)

Rinse salmon; pat dry with paper towels. Combine lemon juice and soy sauce in shallow glass dish. Add salmon; let stand at cool room temperature no more than 15 to 20 minutes, turning salmon several times. Remove salmon from marinade; discard marinade. Season lightly with salt and pepper.

Lightly oil hot grid to prevent sticking. Grill salmon on covered grill over medium KINGSFORD® Briquets 10 to 14 minutes. Halfway through cooking time brush salmon with barbecue sauce, then turn and continue grilling until fish flakes when tested with fork. Remove fish from grill; brush with remaining barbecue sauce. Garnish with oregano sprigs and mushrooms, if desired.

Makes 4 servings

Fish

Snapper with Pesto Butter

½ cup butter or margarine, softened
1 cup packed fresh basil leaves, coarsely chopped *or* ½ cup chopped fresh parsley plus 2 tablespoons dried basil leaves, crushed
3 tablespoons finely grated fresh Parmesan cheese
1 clove garlic, minced
Olive oil
2 to 3 teaspoons lemon juice
4 to 6 red snapper, rock cod, salmon or other medium-firm fish fillets (at least ½ inch thick)
Salt and black pepper
Lemon wedges

To make Pesto Butter, place butter, basil, cheese, garlic and 1 tablespoon oil in blender or food processor; process until blended. Stir in lemon juice to taste. Rinse fish; pat dry with paper towels. Brush one side of fish lightly with oil; season with salt and pepper.

Lightly oil hot grid to prevent sticking. Grill fillets, oil sides down, on covered grill, over medium KINGSFORD® Briquets, 5 to 9 minutes. Halfway through cooking time, brush tops with oil; season with salt and pepper. Turn and continue grilling until fish turns opaque throughout. (Allow 3 to 5 minutes for each ½ inch of thickness.) Serve each fillet with spoonful of Pesto Butter and wedge of lemon.   *Makes 4 to 6 servings*

Fish

Grilled Fish Steaks with Tomato Basil Butter Sauce

Tomato Basil Butter Sauce (recipe page 46)
4 fish steaks, such as halibut, swordfish, tuna or salmon (at least ¾ inch thick)
Olive oil
Salt and black pepper
Fresh basil leaves and summer squash slices for garnish
Hot cooked seasoned noodles (optional)

Prepare Tomato Basil Butter Sauce; set aside. Rinse fish; pat dry with paper towels. Brush one side of fish lightly with oil; season with salt and pepper.

Lightly oil hot grid to prevent sticking. Grill fish, oil sides down, on covered grill, over medium KINGSFORD® Briquets, 6 to 10 minutes. Halfway through cooking time, brush top with oil and season with salt and pepper, then turn and continue grilling until fish turns from translucent to opaque throughout. (Grilling time depends on the thickness of fish; allow 3 to 5 minutes for each ½ inch of thickness.) Serve with Tomato Basil Butter Sauce. Garnish with basil leaves and squash slices. Serve with noodles, if desired.

Makes 4 servings

Fish

37

Tuna Vera Cruz

3 tablespoons tequila, rum or vodka
2 tablespoons lime juice
2 teaspoons grated lime peel
1 piece (1-inch cube) fresh ginger, minced
2 cloves garlic, minced
1 teaspoon salt
1 teaspoon sugar
½ teaspoon ground cumin
¼ teaspoon ground cinnamon
¼ teaspoon black pepper
1 tablespoon vegetable oil
1½ pounds fresh tuna, halibut, swordfish
    or shark steaks
    Lemon and lime wedges
    Fresh rosemary sprigs

Combine tequila, lime juice, lime peel, ginger,
garlic, salt, sugar, cumin, cinnamon and pepper
in 2-quart glass dish; stir in oil. Add tuna; turn
to coat. Cover and refrigerate at least 30 minutes.
Remove tuna from marinade; discard marinade.

Lightly oil hot grid to prevent sticking. Grill tuna
over medium-hot KINGSFORD® Briquets about
4 minutes per side until fish flakes when tested
with fork. Garnish with lemon wedges, lime
wedges and rosemary sprigs.

Makes 4 servings

Fish

Grilled Fish with Orange-Chile Salsa

3 medium oranges, peeled and
    sectioned* (about 1¼ cups segments)
¼ cup finely diced green, red or yellow
    bell pepper
3 tablespoons chopped cilantro, divided
3 tablespoons lime juice, divided
1 tablespoon honey
1 teaspoon minced seeded serrano
    pepper *or* 1 tablespoon minced
    jalapeño pepper**
1¼ pounds firm white fish fillets, such as
    red snapper, halibut or orange
    roughy
    Lime slices (optional)

*Canned mandarin orange segments can be substituted for
fresh orange segments, if desired.

**Chile peppers can sting and irritate the skin; wear rubber
gloves when handling peppers and do not touch your eyes.
Wash hands after handling peppers.

To prepare Orange-Chile Salsa, combine orange
segments, bell pepper, 2 tablespoons cilantro,
2 tablespoons lime juice, honey and serrano
pepper. Set aside.

Season fish fillets with remaining 1 tablespoon
cilantro and 1 tablespoon lime juice. Lightly oil
grid to prevent sticking. Grill fish on covered grill
over medium KINGSFORD® Briquets 5 minutes.
Turn and top with lime slices, if desired. Grill
about 5 minutes until fish flakes easily when tested
with fork. Serve with Orange-Chile Salsa.

Makes 4 servings

Note: *Allow about 10 minutes grilling time per
inch thickness of fish fillets.*

Fish

39

Salmon, Asparagus and Shiitake Salad

¼ cup cider vinegar
¼ cup extra-virgin olive oil
    Grated peel and juice of 1 lemon
4 teaspoons Dijon mustard, divided
1 clove garlic, minced
¼ teaspoon salt
¼ teaspoon black pepper
2 teaspoons minced fresh tarragon or
    ¾ teaspoon dried tarragon leaves
1 pound small salmon fillets, skinned
1 medium red onion, thinly sliced
1 pound asparagus, ends trimmed
¼ pound shiitake mushrooms or button
    mushrooms
    Additional salt and black pepper
8 cups lightly packed torn romaine and
    red leaf lettuce

To prepare dressing, combine vinegar, oil, lemon peel, juice, 2 teaspoons mustard, garlic, ¼ teaspoon salt and ¼ teaspoon pepper in medium bowl; spoon 3 tablespoons dressing into 2-quart glass dish to use as marinade. Reserve remaining dressing. Add tarragon and 2 teaspoons remaining mustard to marinade in glass dish; blend well. Add salmon; turn to coat. Cover and refrigerate 1 hour. Transfer

3 tablespoons reserved dressing to medium bowl; add onion, tossing to coat. Thread asparagus and mushrooms onto wooden skewers. (Soak skewers in hot water 30 minutes to prevent burning.)

Remove salmon from marinade; discard marinade. Season salmon with additional salt and pepper. Lightly oil hot grid to prevent sticking. Grill salmon over medium-hot KINGSFORD® Briquets 2 to 4 minutes per side or until fish flakes when tested with fork. Grill asparagus and mushrooms over medium-hot briquets 5 to 8 minutes or until crisp-tender. Cut asparagus into 2-inch pieces and slice mushrooms; add to onion mixture. Let stand 10 minutes. Toss lettuce with onion mixture in large bowl; arrange lettuce mixture on platter. Break salmon into 2-inch pieces; arrange salmon over lettuce mixture. Drizzle with remaining reserved dressing. Serve immediately.

Makes 4 main-dish servings

Shrimp Skewers with Tropical Fruit Salsa

½ **cup soy sauce**
¼ **cup lime juice**
2 **cloves garlic, minced**
1½ **pounds large shrimp, shelled and deveined**
   Tropical Fruit Salsa (recipe page 43)
   Vegetable oil
   Salt and black pepper

Combine soy sauce, lime juice and garlic in shallow glass dish or large resealable plastic food storage bag. Add shrimp; cover dish or seal bag. Marinate in refrigerator no longer than 30 minutes.

Meanwhile, prepare Tropical Fruit Salsa. (Salsa should not be made more than two hours before serving.)

Remove shrimp from marinade; discard marinade. Thread shrimp onto metal or bamboo skewers. (Soak bamboo skewers in water 20 minutes to prevent burning.) Brush one side of shrimp lightly with oil; season with salt and pepper.

Lightly oil hot grid to prevent sticking. Grill shrimp, oil sides down, on covered grill, over medium-hot KINGSFORD® Briquets, 6 to 8 minutes. Halfway through cooking time, brush top with oil, season with salt and pepper, then turn and continue grilling until shrimp firm up and turn opaque throughout. Serve with Tropical Fruit Salsa.

Makes 4 servings

Shrimp

Tropical Fruit Salsa

- **2 mangos***
- **2 kiwifruit**
- **3 tablespoons finely chopped or finely slivered red onion**
- **3 tablespoons lime juice**
- **¼ teaspoon salt**
- **⅓ teaspoon crushed red pepper flakes**
- **1 teaspoon sugar**
- **1 tablespoon finely chopped fresh mint leaves**
- **1 tablespoon finely chopped fresh cilantro**

Substitute 1 papaya or 2 large or 3 medium peaches for mangos.

Peel fruit. Cut mango into ¼-inch pieces; cut kiwifruit into wedges. Combine with remaining ingredients in medium bowl; adjust flavors to taste. Cover and refrigerate 2 hours.

Makes about 1 cup

Tip: *Mangos are available most of the year in many large supermarkets. They are ripe when they yield to gentle pressure; color of skin does not indicate ripeness. Unripe mangos will ripen in a few days when stored at room temperature. To dice fruit, first peel skin, then cut fruit lengthwise away from seed, then cut crosswise into ¼-inch pieces.*

Cajun Grilled Shrimp

3 green onions, minced
2 tablespoons lemon juice
3 cloves garlic, minced
2 teaspoons paprika
1 teaspoon salt
¼ to ½ teaspoon black pepper
¼ to ½ teaspoon cayenne pepper
1 tablespoon olive oil
1½ pounds shrimp, shelled with tails intact,
   deveined
Lemon wedges

Combine onions, lemon juice, garlic, paprika, salt and peppers in 2-quart glass dish; stir in oil. Add shrimp; turn to coat. Cover and refrigerate at least 15 minutes. Thread shrimp onto metal or wooden skewers. (Soak wooden skewers in hot water 30 minutes to prevent burning.)

Lightly oil hot grid to prevent sticking. Grill shrimp over medium-hot KINGSFORD® Briquets about 2 minutes per side until opaque. Serve immediately with lemon wedges.

Makes 4 servings

Shrimp

Grilled Garlic

1 or 2 heads garlic
Olive oil

Peel outermost papery skin from garlic heads.
Brush heads with oil. Grill heads at edge of grid
on covered grill over medium-hot KINGSFORD®
Briquets 30 to 45 minutes or until cloves are soft
and buttery. Remove from grill; cool slightly.
Gently squeeze softened garlic head from root end
so that cloves slip out of skins into small bowl. Use
immediately or cover and refrigerate up to
1 week.

Citrus Tarragon Butter

  ½ **cup butter, softened**
   1 **tablespoon finely chopped fresh**
     tarragon
   1 **tablespoon lemon juice**
   1 **tablespoon orange juice**
   1 **teaspoon finely grated orange peel**
   1 **teaspoon finely grated lemon peel**

Beat butter in a small bowl until soft and light. Stir
in remaining ingredients. Cover and refrigerate
until ready to serve.   *Makes about ½ cup*

Tomato Basil Butter Sauce

4 tablespoons butter or margarine, softened, divided
1½ cups chopped seeded peeled tomatoes (about 1 pound)
½ teaspoon sugar
1 clove garlic, minced
Salt and black pepper
1½ tablespoons very finely chopped fresh basil

Melt 1 tablespoon butter in small skillet. Add tomatoes, sugar and garlic. Cook over medium-low heat, stirring frequently, until liquid evaporates and mixture thickens. Remove pan from heat; stir in remaining butter until mixture has saucelike consistency. Season to taste with salt and pepper, then stir in basil. *Makes about 1 cup*